W9-BAK-822

40

ANIMALS

• HOW THEY WORK •

DAVID BURNIE

STERLING PUBLISHING CO. INC.

NEW YORK

6194492

Editor: Thomas Keegan
Design: David West Children's
Book Design
Illustrators: Karen Johnson and
Caroline Barnard. Subsidiary illustrations
by David Burroughs.

Library of Congress
Cataloging-in-Publication Data Available

10 9 8 7 6 5 4 3 2 1

Published 1994 by Sterling Publishing
Company, Inc.
387 Park Avenue South, New York,
N.Y. 10016
Originally published by
Simon & Schuster Young Books
under the title *Animals by Design*
© 1993 Simon & Schuster Young Books
Distributed in Canada by
Sterling Publishing
℅ Canadian Manda Group,
P.O. Box 920, Station U
Toronto, Ontario, Canada M8Z 5P9

Typeset by Goodfellow and Egan Ltd
Printed and bound in Hong Kong

All rights reserved. No part of this
publication may be reproduced, stored in
a retrieval system, or transmitted in any
form, or by any means, electronic,
mechanical, photocopying, recording or
otherwise, without the prior permission of
the publisher.

Sterling ISBN 0-8069-0742-8

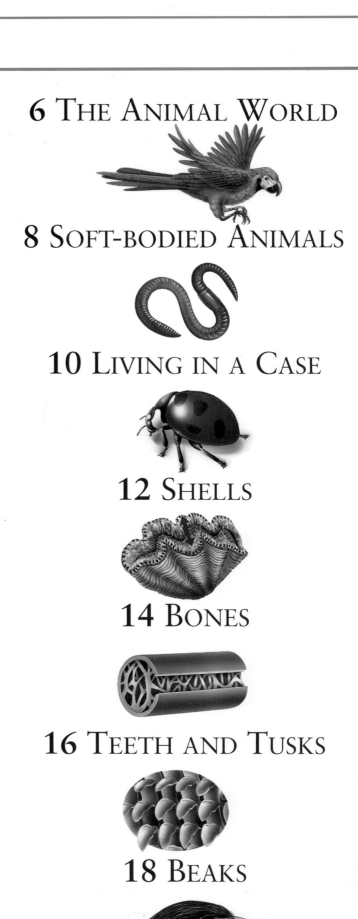

CONTENTS

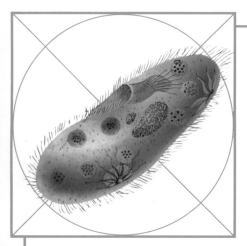

THE ANIMAL WORLD

Animal bodies are like extraordinary and very intricate machines. They have billions of different parts, and all the parts work together to carry out the tasks of staying alive. But machines have to be maintained and supplied with energy, while an animal can do these things for itself. An animal can also sense the world around it, and it can grow and reproduce. Animals gradually change, or evolve, as one generation succeeds another.

Cells

Every animal on Earth is built of cells. Some animals have a single cell. Others have billions, with different types of cells doing different jobs.

Filtering food

Sponges are simple animals made of many cells. Some of the cells work like pumps. They suck in water through holes or pores in the sponge, and filter out any food that it contains.

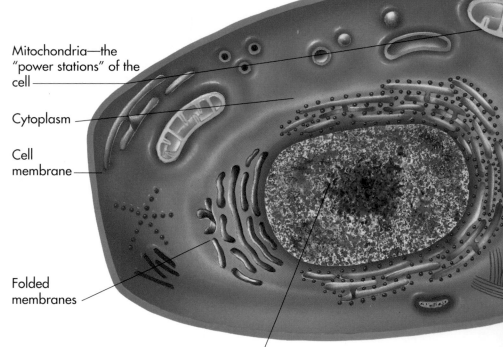

Mitochondria—the "power stations" of the cell

Cytoplasm

Cell membrane

Folded membranes

Nucleus—the cell's control center

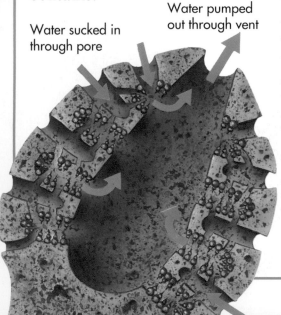

Water pumped out through vent

Water sucked in through pore

Mollusks

A snail is a mollusk, one of 40,000 species which live in water or on land. A snail doesn't have any bones in its body, but it is protected by a hard shell. Mollusks are not the only animals that make shells, but their shells include the biggest and the most elaborate in the animal world. You can find out more about shells on pages 12-13.

Armored insects

A wasp's body is divided into 3 parts—the head, thorax and abdomen—covered with a hard case made up of separate plates. On the wasp's abdomen, these plates can slide over each other like tubes in a telescope. On pages 10-11 you can find out more about body cases, and the animals that have them.

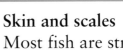
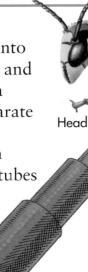

Abdomen

Head

Thorax

Skin and scales

Most fish are streamlined animals, and have bodies that are covered by scales. Fish have existed for over 500 million years, and there are over 20,000 species, making them the most common vertebrates (animals with backbones). Because fish are quite large animals, they have a special way of collecting oxygen. (See page 33.)

Living on land

Reptiles were the first vertebrate animals to make a real success of living on land. Two things helped them to succeed—a thick skin that is covered with scales, and eggs that have shells. On pages 40-41 you can see how eggs develop, and find out why shells are so useful to land animals.

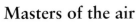

Centriole

Masters of the air

Birds evolved from reptiles. But unlike reptiles, their bodies are "warm-blooded." They stay at the same temperature, whatever the temperature outside. There are about 8,600 species of bird in the world today. They are the most powerful of all flying animals, and they are the only animals that have feathers. On pages 28-29 you can find out how feathers and wings work.

Mammals

Mammals are animals that have hair and that raise their young on milk. They live in almost every habitat on Earth, and are warm-blooded, like birds. Find out more about mammals on pages 20-21.

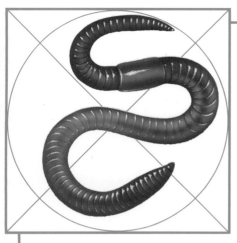

SOFT-BODIED ANIMALS

If you fill a balloon with water, and then tie it so that the water cannot get out, you will have something that is like a soft-bodied animal. Soft-bodied animals do not have bones. Instead, they use the pressure of their body fluids to hold their shape. The fluid presses against the outside of the animal, just like the water presses against the balloon, and this keeps the animal in shape. Soft-bodied animals are very common in the sea. They often have a spreading shape, and the surrounding water helps to support their bodies.

Moving without legs

An earthworm's body is divided up into many separate compartments, or segments. It moves by making the segments change shape. When the segments are short and fat they grip the ground, so that the other parts of the worm can move forward.

More segments contract and grip the ground

Body gradually moves forward

Direction of movement

Tentacles held out by fluid pressure

Mouth

A sea anemone's tentacles use pressure to give them their shape—like a party whistle

Segment about to elongate, pushing head forward

Segment about to contract, pulling tail forward

Deadly tentacles

A sea anemone is a hollow-bodied animal that looks very much like a plant. But there is nothing plant-like about the way that an anemone feeds. It uses its stinging tentacles to catch small animals. It then carries them to its mouth, and into its body cavity. A sea anemone's tentacles are held up by the pressure of fluid inside them. If an anemone is uncovered by the tide, it cannot hold its tentacles up, and they collapse. Most anemones pull them in before this happens.

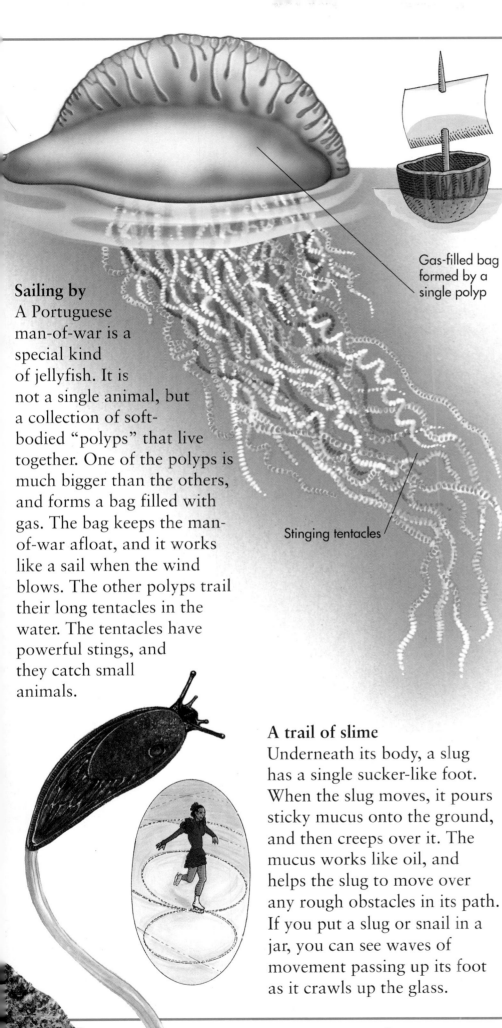

Lights in the sea
A comb jelly is a small, almost transparent animal with two long tentacles. Each tentacle has very fine branches, which catch small pieces of food. Comb jellies flicker with green light after dark.

Gas-filled bag formed by a single polyp

Sailing by
A Portuguese man-of-war is a special kind of jellyfish. It is not a single animal, but a collection of soft-bodied "polyps" that live together. One of the polyps is much bigger than the others, and forms a bag filled with gas. The bag keeps the man-of-war afloat, and it works like a sail when the wind blows. The other polyps trail their long tentacles in the water. The tentacles have powerful stings, and they catch small animals.

Stinging tentacles

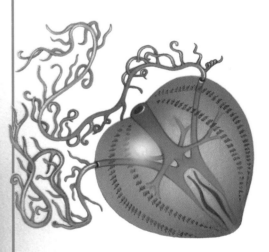

Living sieve
An adult sea-squirt has a body that works like a living sieve. It pumps water in through a special hole, or siphon, using small tentacles, and then pumps it out through another, filtering out food on the way.

A trail of slime
Underneath its body, a slug has a single sucker-like foot. When the slug moves, it pours sticky mucus onto the ground, and then creeps over it. The mucus works like oil, and helps the slug to move over any rough obstacles in its path. If you put a slug or snail in a jar, you can see waves of movement passing up its foot as it crawls up the glass.

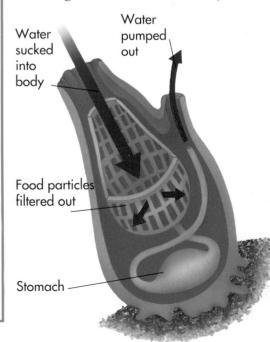

Water pumped out

Water sucked into body

Food particles filtered out

Stomach

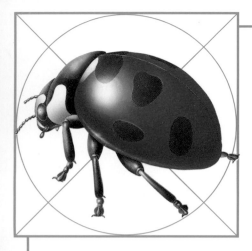

LIVING IN A CASE

Like all mammals, we have skeletons that are inside our bodies (see p.14). But many small animals are not like this. Instead, their bodies are arranged the other way around. They have a hard case on the outside, which protects the soft body parts on the inside. Either the case can be made of a single piece of something hard, or it can be made of lots of smaller pieces that join together. Body cases are very strong, but they have two disadvantages: they make growing difficult, and large body cases are awkward to carry around.

Making things move

The separate plates of a beetle's body case are hard, but the places where they meet —called joints—are much softer. At each joint, the beetle has a set of muscles that can pull one plate against its neighbor. By doing this, it is able to make its body move. If you look closely at the leg of a beetle or a grasshopper, you should be able to see its joints. The feet have lots of joints close together, so they can move in almost any direction. The hard shell covers the wings. These are also powered by the action of the plates.

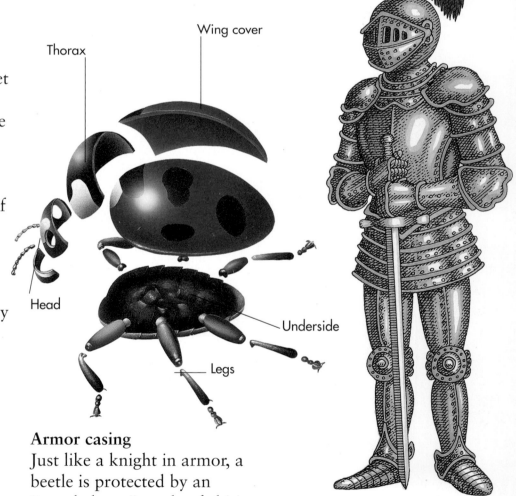

Thorax

Wing cover

Head

Underside

Legs

Armor casing

Just like a knight in armor, a beetle is protected by an "exoskeleton" made of chitin. Chitin is very strong and also waterproof, which helps to keep the beetle from drying out. Two big plates cover its wings. Others cover its head and underside, and tube-like plates cover its legs and feet.

Cups of stone

Coral polyps are small animals that catch food with a ring of tentacles. They usually feed at night. During the day they protect themselves by pulling their tentacles inside a stony cup. Some coral polyps live so close together that their cups join up to make a branching "skeleton." As the polyps grow and die, the pile of skeletons they leave behind gets bigger and bigger, and the result is a coral reef. The world's biggest reef—the Great Barrier Reef of Australia—is over 1,250 miles (2,000 km) long.

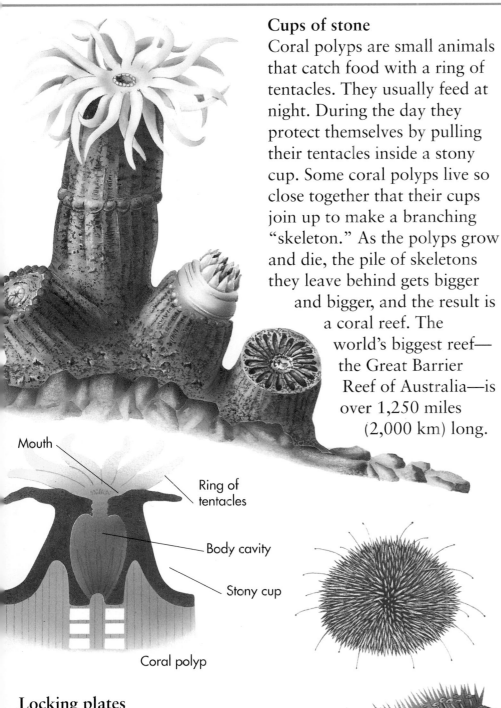

Mouth

Ring of tentacles

Body cavity

Stony cup

Coral polyp

Locking plates

The body of a sea-urchin is covered with hundreds of small, chalky plates. Some of the plates carry long spines, while others have tiny pincers that can clean the spines or fend off small animals. The sea-urchin's case is also covered with a thin layer of living cells, so it lies just inside its body, rather than outside it.

Mollusk shells

The bodies of most mollusks —or "shellfish"—are protected by a hard shell. Snails and limpets have a single shell, while mussels and oysters have a shell made of two parts. Chitons are mollusks that have a shell made up of 8 separate pieces.

Tailor-made case

The larvae (grubs) of caddisflies live underwater. They are protected by cases which they make by glueing together pieces of wood, tiny shells or sand grains.

Changing up

Many animals with hard body cases "molt" as they grow, shedding their body case to replace it with a bigger one. The new case is soft but soon hardens.

SHELLS

A shell is a special kind of protective case. Most shells are made by soft-bodied animals called mollusks, which include snails, cockles and cuttlefish. They make them from a common mineral called calcium carbonate, collecting it from the water around them, or from their food, and turning it into crystals, which they arrange in a particular way. As a mollusk grows, it adds crystals to the edge of the shell, so that it grows too. You can often see these growth ridges or bands on shells.

Giant of the reefs

The giant clam has a monster shell that can measure over 1 yard (1m) across. This huge animal lives in coral reefs, and is the world's biggest "bivalve" mollusk. Bivalves have a shell made of two parts joined by a hinge. The clam can close its shell by using powerful muscles. Stories of divers trapped by giant clams are unproved!

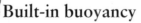
Ballast tank

Built-in buoyancy

A submarine has to be able to travel underwater without floating back to the surface or plunging to the ocean floor. It does this by adjusting the amount of air in special ballast tanks. The pearly nautilus is a mollusk that works in a similar way. Its shell is divided into many gas-filled compartments. The nautilus adjusts the gas pressure so that it floats without rising or falling. The gas pressure inside the shell is much less than the water pressure outside, so the shell has to be very strong.

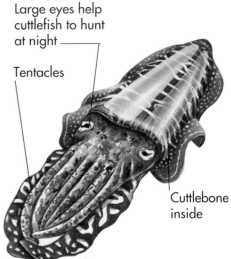

A living drill
The shipworm is not a real worm, but a mollusk with a small, sharp-edged shell. It uses its shell to bore through wood, and feeds on the wood particles. Like all animals, the shipworm needs oxygen, which it gets by pumping water through siphons. Mooring posts and boat hulls can be badly damaged by shipworms.

Braving the waves
Even the fiercest storm cannot dislodge a limpet from its rocky home. Limpets have very strong, cone-shaped shells, and a single foot like a powerful sucker. At the first sign of danger, a limpet clamps its shell to the rock.

Right-hand thread
What have a tower shell and a wood screw got in common? A right-hand thread! If you hold a shell or screw so that it points away from you, the spiral turns clockwise, or away right. Almost all mollusks that have spiral shells turn in the same way. The tightness of the spiral gives a shell its characteristic shape.

Bubble raft
The violet sea snail is a traveler of the open sea. It produces lots of mucus filled with air bubbles. The bubbly mucus turns hard, making a raft that the snail can hang from. Violet sea snails feed on other small animals that float on the sea's surface.

Large eyes help cuttlefish to hunt at night

Tentacles

Cuttlebone inside

Inside shell
A cuttlefish is a mollusk that has a flattened shell inside its body, called a cuttlebone. This is filled with spaces that are separated by tiny struts. The spaces contain air, and they work like a float. The cuttlefish hunts at night. At dawn, it floods some of the cuttlebone spaces with water, and sinks to the ocean floor.

BONES

Bones are like scaffolding. They support an animal's body from inside and provide something solid that its muscles can pull against. Bones cannot bend, but their positions can be changed. This happens at flexible junctions, called joints, which are between the bones. We have over 200 bones in our bodies, varying greatly in size. The smallest are in our ears, the largest in our legs.

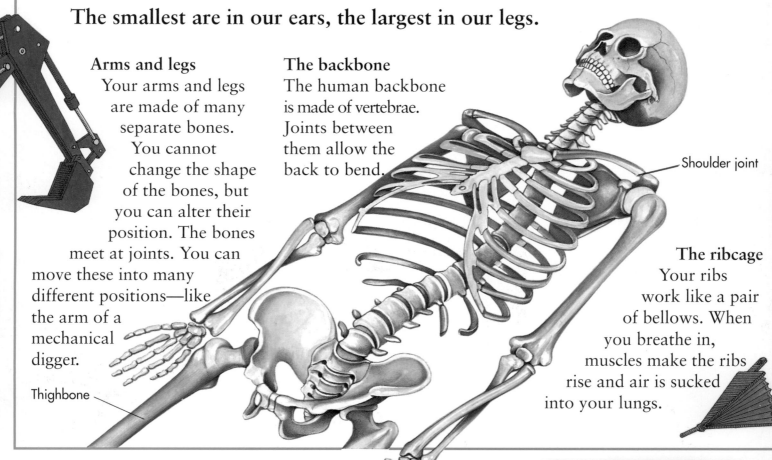

Arms and legs
Your arms and legs are made of many separate bones. You cannot change the shape of the bones, but you can alter their position. The bones meet at joints. You can move these into many different positions—like the arm of a mechanical digger.

Thighbone

The backbone
The human backbone is made of vertebrae. Joints between them allow the back to bend.

Shoulder joint

The ribcage
Your ribs work like a pair of bellows. When you breathe in, muscles make the ribs rise and air is sucked into your lungs.

Light for flight
A bird's wing bones have to be light, but they also need to be strong and stiff. The longest bones in bird wings are hollow. They are filled with air, and they also have many small struts that give them added strength. Criss-cross struts in an aircraft give lightness and strength in the same way.

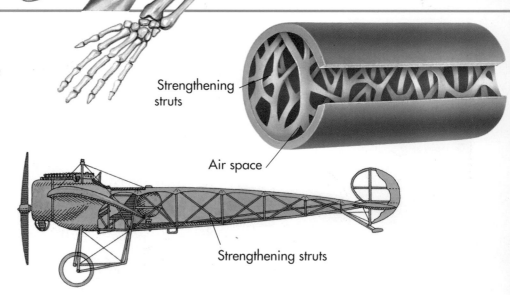

Strengthening struts

Air space

Strengthening struts

The skull
Your skull is a complicated collection of twenty-two bones. Eight of the bones make a box called the cranium, which protects your brain. The others form your face and inner ears. Your brain is surrounded by fluid which works like a shock absorber to protect your brain from knocks.

Cartilage
Cartilage is a strong and flexible substance rather like plastic. It is found in joints, where it helps bones to slide over each other. Your backbone is made of many separate bones, called vertebrae, that are separated by disks of cartilage. Most animals have bone and cartilage in their skeletons, but sharks have just cartilage.

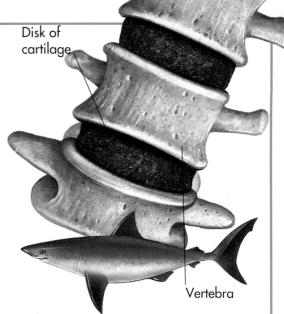

Disk of cartilage

Vertebra

Locked together
Your cranium has joints called sutures. When the skull forms, the bones grow till they fit together like a jigsaw.

Hinge joint
The elbow is a hinge joint. It moves up and down, but not sideways. Bones of moving joints are tipped with cartilage and oiled with a special fluid.

Ball-and-socket joint
At the hip joint, the ball-shaped end of your thigh bone fits into a rounded socket. This kind of joint can move in almost any direction.

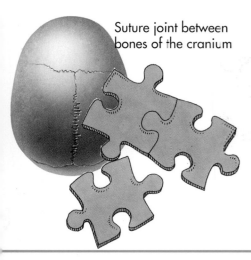

Suture joint between bones of the cranium

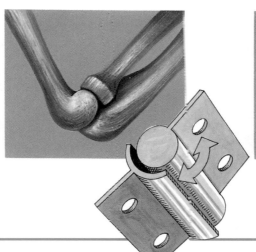

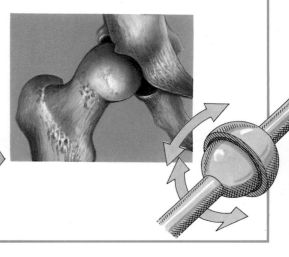

Bones for hearing
Deep inside your ear are 3 tiny bones. They are called the hammer, anvil and stirrup after their shape. The hammer is attached to the eardrum. It moves the two other bones when the eardrum is vibrated by sound. The stirrup passes the movement to the inner ear, where special cells detect it.

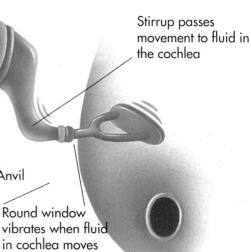

Stirrup passes movement to fluid in the cochlea

Hammer moves when eardrum vibrates

Anvil

Eardrum vibrates when sound waves reach the ear

Round window vibrates when fluid in cochlea moves

TEETH AND TUSKS

Few parts of your body get as much wear as your teeth. They cut or grind their way through the toughest kinds of food, and they have to withstand immense pressure without cracking. Humans have just two sets of teeth. Once a tooth has "erupted" or appeared, it does not grow any bigger. But the teeth of other animals often work in a different way. Some animals have teeth that keep growing all the time, so that they never wear away. Others have teeth that form on a non-stop production line. Each tooth has a short life, but as soon as its time is finished, another tooth is ready to take its place.

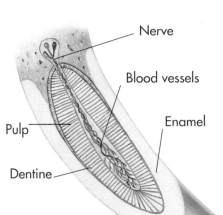

Nerve

Blood vessels

Enamel

Pulp

Dentine

Inside a tooth
Teeth and tusks are made of soft pulp, covered with enamel —the hardest substance in the body.

Non-stop teeth
A shark's teeth do not grow inside its jaws, like ours. They form behind the jaws, lying flat. Each tooth slowly moves forwards, and gradually becomes upright. After a while, it falls out, and is replaced by the tooth behind it. Sharks' teeth can be over 2 1/2 inches (6 cm) long.

Human teeth

Your teeth work like a set of tools, and each kind of tooth has a different job. Incisors, at the front of your mouth, cut into food when you bite. Your canines help you to grip what you are eating, and your molars grind it up. The first set of teeth, called the milk teeth or deciduous teeth, is made up of 8 incisors, 4 canines and just 8 molars. These are gradually replaced by the permanent teeth. Most people have thirty-two permanent teeth.

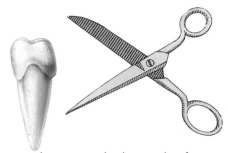

Incisors have a single sharp edge for cutting

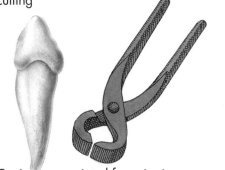

Canines are pointed for gripping

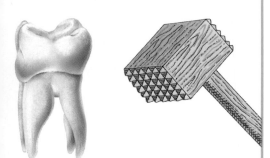

Molars have flat tops for crushing, and long roots

Cutting through wood

A beaver chisels its way through wood. Its incisors never stop growing, so they never wear out. Many small mammals, including mice, have similar incisors.

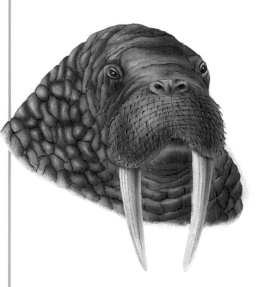

The strangest whale

The narwhal is a small whale that lives in the Arctic Ocean. Male narwhals are unique in the animal world. Their single, spiral tusk is an incisor.

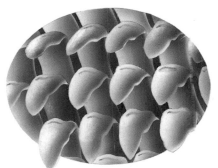

Deadly teeth

The puff adder has long hollow teeth, or fangs, that swing forward when it is about to bite. The fangs work like syringes, injecting a powerful poison into the prey. Rattlesnakes have the same kind of fangs. The fangs of cobras and sea snakes do not have hinges and stay upright.

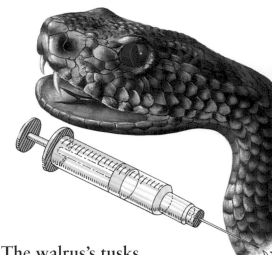

The walrus's tusks

A walrus has two long tusks that grow from its upper jaw. The tusks are special canine teeth, and in males they can grow nearly 1 yard (1m) long. Walruses use their tusks to gouge mollusks from the soft ocean floor, and also to attack their enemies.

A snail's teeth

Snails have hundreds of teeth, so small that you would need a microscope to see them. They use their teeth to scrape at plants, and sometimes leave zigzag toothmarks.

BEAKS

If you imagine living with your hands tied behind your back, you will see why beaks are so important to birds. A bird cannot use its wings to hold or grip anything, or even to scratch itself. It has to do all these things either with its beak, or with its feet. There are over 8,600 species of bird in the world, and each has a beak that is shaped to suit its style of life. All beaks have a framework of bone covered with keratin—the same substance that makes up our fingernails.

Beautiful beak
A toucan's brightly colored beak can be almost as long as its body. The toucan uses it like a giant pair of tweezers to collect fruit in its home in the treetops. Although the beak looks very heavy, the inside is built like a honeycomb and is full of air spaces. There are over thirty species of toucan, and they all have different beak patterns. This one is a toco toucan.

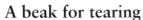

A beak for tearing
Hunting birds, like eagles and owls, feed on meat. But like all birds, they have no teeth and cannot chew their food. Instead, hunting birds have beaks that end with a sharp hook. They use it to tear their food up.

Sieving a meal

The flamingo feeds with its head upside down, and its beak dipped in water. Its beak works like a combined pump and sieve. The lower half of the beak pumps water through fibers on the upper half of its beak and its tongue. The fibres catch tiny animals and plants, and the flamingo swallows them.

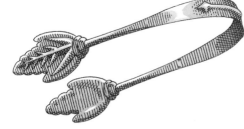

Mid-air refueling

Eating on the wing is not a problem for hummingbirds. These tiny birds feed on nectar, which is a sugary liquid made by flowers. A hummingbird buzzes between flowers like an insect, and hovers in front of each one while it inserts its long beak. The two parts of the hummingbird's beak fit together to make a tube like a drinking straw. The bird sucks up the nectar, and moves on for its next meal.

Spooning it up

The spoonbill is a long-legged bird that wades in shallow water. Its strangely shaped beak looks quite unwieldy, but it is a very effective tool for catching small animals underwater. The spoonbill hunts by walking forward slowly, with its beak dipped beneath the water's surface. It holds the two halves of its beak open like a pair of tongs and moves its head from side to side. If a small animal touches its beak, the spoonbill feels it straight away, and snaps its beak shut. Because spoonbills hunt by touch rather than by sight, they can catch food in muddy water.

Cutting a hole

A woodpecker hammers at tree trunks to get at wood-boring insects, and also to call to other woodpeckers. As well as having a long, sharp beak, a woodpecker also has an amazingly long tongue with a sticky tip, which it uses to pull out the insect.

SKIN, HAIR AND FUR

No matter how careful you are with your clothes, they will not last for ever. But the barrier that protects your body—the skin—is much stronger than clothing. Skin never wears out. If it gets stretched it springs back, and if it gets scratched or cut, it repairs itself. Skin protects the body from injury, and it keeps out harmful bacteria. It also helps warm-blooded animals, like ourselves, to stay at the right temperature. Hair, fur and feathers work like a blanket, holding in the body's heat, while sweat glands cool the body.

Hair

Hair keeps us warm, and also keeps dust out of our eyes and noses. A hair is made of dead cells, and it grows from a special pit in the skin. Hair from different animals often looks very different when it is magnified.

Feeling cold

When you feel cold, tiny muscles make the hairs in your skin stand upright and the blood vessels in the skin narrow to keep warm blood away from your skin so that your body loses less heat.

Cat hair

Horse hair

Bat hair

Hairs are covered with tiny scales. The pattern made by the scales is different for every type of mammal

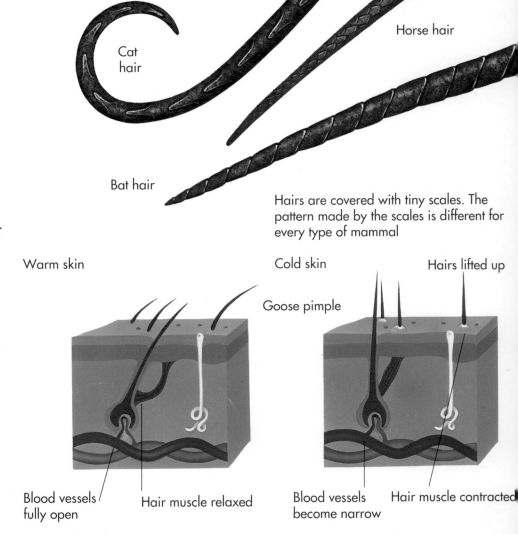

Warm skin

Cold skin

Goose pimple

Hairs lifted up

Blood vessels fully open

Hair muscle relaxed

Blood vessels become narrow

Hair muscle contracted

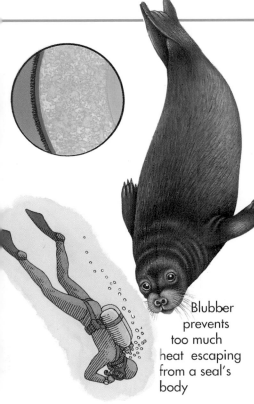

A jacket of fat

Whales and seals are mammals. Like all mammals, their bodies have to stay warm to work properly. But whales and seals live in places where the water temperature is as low as 39°F (4°C)— about the same as in a refrigerator. They keep their bodies warm with a thick layer of fat, called blubber.

Blubber prevents too much heat escaping from a seal's body

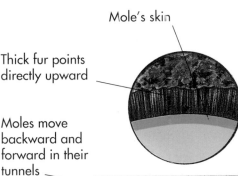

The mole's velvet jacket

Most mammals have hair that points down their bodies, from their head to their legs. If you look at the hair on your arms, you will see that it also points in a particular direction. But a mole's velvety fur is different. It points straight upward enabling the mole to move forward and backward in its tunnels without brushing its fur the wrong way and clogging it with earth.

Mole's skin

Thick fur points directly upward

Moles move backward and forward in their tunnels

Winter warmer

Many mammals have fur made of two types of hair. They have long, coarse "guard" hairs and short wool hairs, which are softer. Sheep have been bred so that their wool hairs are very long. The wool grows non-stop to make a thick fleece. After a sheep is shorn, the separate wool hairs are spun together to make yarn.

Scaly skin

Nearly all reptiles, including lizards, are covered in thick scales. The scales are made of the same substance that forms our nails and hair. They protect a reptile's body and help keep it from losing water. Each scale is hard and stiff, but the skin between the scales is much softer. This allows the skin to stretch and fold when the animal moves. The shape of a lizard's scales varies in different parts of its body. Its head is covered with a few big scales. The scales on the rest of its body are smaller.

Hard scale

Flexible skin between scales

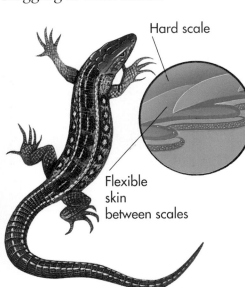

Sliding through the water

A fish's skin is very slippery, allowing it to slide through the water with little effort. The skin is covered by thin scales that overlap like roof tiles. They point backward, so that the water flows past easily. The fish "oils" its scales with mucus.

ANIMAL ARMOR

When faced by danger, many animals run away or hide. Others hold their ground and use their built-in armor as a defense. Some of these animals have strong shells (pages 12-13) that can protect them in an emergency. Others, like the armadillo and woodlouse, have armor that is made up of a number of separate plates. When danger strikes, they roll up so all the vulnerable parts of their body are hidden. A few, like the porcupine, have developed armor that can harm their enemies.

Mobile home

The shell of a turtle or tortoise is a bony box covered with large scales. Most turtles can pull their heads into their shells, and tortoises can usually fold up their legs as well. Tortoises move slowly because their shells are quite heavy, but turtles can move faster in the water.

Rolling into a ball

If you tap a pillbug on its back, it will roll up into a ball for protection. Its hard outer case guards the softer parts of its body, which are safely tucked up inside. Armadillos are unusual mammals that react to danger in the same way. An armadillo's back is covered with hard scales, and so too is the top of its head and tail. When it rolls up, its head and tail fit together to make the ball complete. Hedgehogs curl up, too, but

Armadillo curled into a ball, and protected by scales

Pillbug curled into a ball, and protected by body case

Hedgehog curled up with spines sticking out

their bodies are covered with spines rather than scales. A hedgehog makes its spines stand on end when it curls up.

Armor-plated rhinos

Rhinoceroses have very thick and almost hairless skin. The skin of some rhinos is flat, but the skin of an Indian rhino is folded into sheets, which look just like armor plating. A rhino's skin protects it from the bites of other animals both big and small. Unfortunately, it does not protect it from poachers, who hunt it for its horns.

Backing out of trouble

If a porcupine is threatened by another animal, it turns its back on its attacker, and shakes its quills so that they rattle. Usually this warning sign is enough to put off its enemy. If not, it makes a backward charge. Its quills pull out easily, and stick in its enemy.

Hard plate reinforced by calcium carbonate

Changing armor

A crab's body case is reinforced with crystals of calcium carbonate, which makes it very hard. The separate plates that form the case are linked by flexible joints, just like the parts of a deep-sea diving suit. Normally, the crab is well protected by its armor. But as it grows, it has to keep replacing its case with a bigger one. For a while, the new case is quite soft, so the crab has to hide away until its armor has hardened.

Flexible joint between plates

An unappetizing meal

Life is not easy for a caterpillar. It has to feed almost non-stop, but all the time it risks being seen and eaten by birds. Some caterpillars are armed with special hairs. If a bird attacks a caterpillar like this, it soon spits it out.

LEGS, FEET AND HANDS

When people take photographs, they sometimes steady the camera with a 3-legged stand called a tripod. There are no 3-legged animals in the world, but there are a great many that have 4 legs. These animals are called tetrapods. We humans are tetrapods, even though we only use two of our legs for walking. So too are elephants, lizards, frogs and even birds. Invertebrate animals (ones that do not have backbones) often have more legs than this. All insects have 6 legs, while crabs and lobsters have ten. Millipedes may have as many as 750!

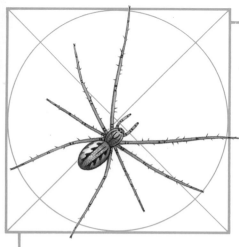

Praying mantis

Deadly legs

A praying mantis has 6 legs, like all insects. The legs are attached to its thorax (the middle part of its body). The mantis uses its middle and back legs to stand on, but it uses its powerful front legs to catch other insects. Each front leg has two rows of sharp spines, which can be pressed together. When the mantis spots a likely victim, it shoots its front legs forward, and then folds them up. The spines grip the insect tightly.

Holding up the body

A mammal's legs support its body from underneath, like the legs of a table. This means that its body is usually kept off the ground.

A reptile's legs work in a different way. They spread out sideways and support it like a stretcher.

Elephant

Crocodile

How legs work

Our legs are like levers. They have sets of muscles that pull against each other, making the leg bones swing in one direction and then back again. A kangaroo's legs work in the same way, except that they have tendons that are very good at storing energy. When a kangaroo lands after a leap, its tendons stretch like pieces of elastic. They help to catapult the kangaroo forward when it takes its next jump. Invertebrates (animals without backbones) have quite different legs.

Rows of tube feet on underside of leg

Stretchy tendons link the kangaroo's muscles to its leg bones

Tentacles with suckers on the underside

Camel

Gibbon

Gecko

Falcon

Hands and feet

Humans belong to a group of animals, called primates, which also includes apes and monkeys. Primates are the only animals that have hands. Hands have thumbs, which enable us to grip something or to turn it around. Most other 4-legged animals have 4 similar feet, which are shaped to suit the way that they move. A camel's feet spread its weight, so that it does not sink in sand. A gecko's toes have pads which grip like velcro. A bird's "forelimbs" are its wings. Some use their feet to catch prey.

25

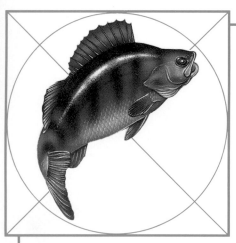

PADDLES, FINS AND FLIPPERS

A boat moves through the water by pushing backward with its propeller. As the water moves towards the stern, it creates a force that drives the boat in the opposite direction. Water animals also move by pushing water behind them. But instead of using propellers that turn around, most of them use paddles, fins and flippers which beat in one direction and then another. The fish's tail provides the power as it flicks from one side to the other. This movement drives it forward and it steers with its fins.

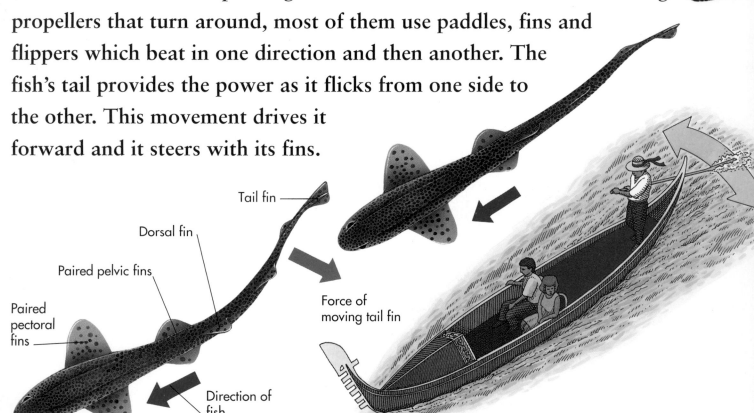

Tail fin

Dorsal fin

Paired pelvic fins

Paired pectoral fins

Force of moving tail fin

Direction of fish

How fish swim
Fish usually have several fins, but most use just their tail fin to move forward. When a fish swims, it flicks its tail sideways and backward against the water to move forward. Fish use their other fins for steering and turning on the spot. Most kinds of fish have fins reinforced by bony "rays." These open and close the fin like a fan.

"Flying" through the sea
Rays have very flat bodies and broad pectoral fins. They flap their way through the water rather like birds flying through the air. Together with their relatives the sharks, rays make up a group of about 600 species called cartilaginous fish. Their skeletons are made of cartilage instead of bone. The biggest ray is the gigantic, but harmless, manta, which can measure up to 20 feet (6.5m) from tip to tip.

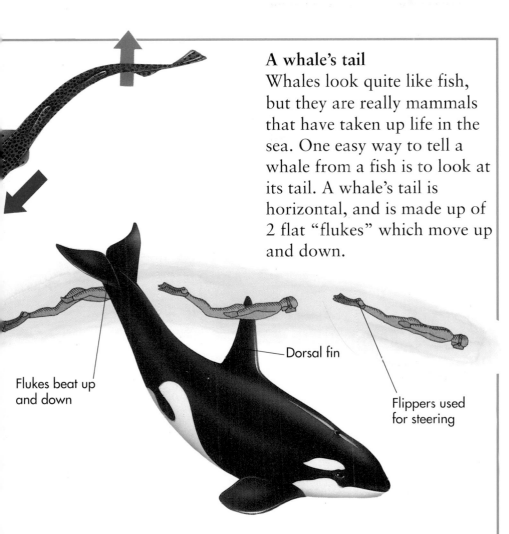

A whale's tail

Whales look quite like fish, but they are really mammals that have taken up life in the sea. One easy way to tell a whale from a fish is to look at its tail. A whale's tail is horizontal, and is made up of 2 flat "flukes" which move up and down.

Flukes beat up and down

Dorsal fin

Flippers used for steering

Slow coach of the seas

Seahorses are some of the strangest fish in the sea. They swim with their bodies upright, and they often anchor themselves by wrapping their flexible tails around pieces of seaweed. They are also the slowest swimmers of all fish. A seahorse pushes itself along by beating its dorsal fin, and it can take about 3 or 4 minutes to swim just 1 yard (1m). Tiny pectoral fins just behind a seahorse's head help it to maneuver.

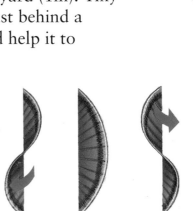

Movement of a seahorse's pectoral fin, seen from behind

Jet propulsion

The squid's body contains a cavity filled with water. The squid can squirt water forward through a tube called a siphon. The force of the water works like air leaving a jet engine, and it drives the squid in the opposite direction.

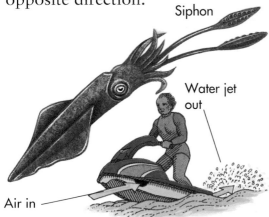

Siphon

Water jet out

Air in

Rowing through the water

A ragworm's body is divided into many segments. Each segment has 2 flaps, which are stiffened by special rods, and a collection of bristles. The flaps work like oars. When the ragworm wriggles its body, they push it through the water. The worm can also use its flaps to walk across the sandy ocean floor.

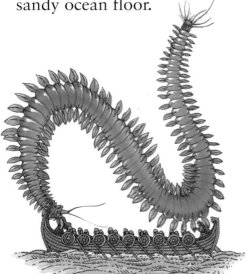

WINGS

Aircraft fly in 2 different ways. Some move through the air under their own power and can stay airborne for a long time. Others just glide through the air and sooner or later fall back to the ground. Animals fly in the same two ways. Many kinds of animals can glide, but only insects, bats and birds can keep themselves in the air using their own muscle power. Insects are nature's smallest fliers. They have stiff wings, made of the same substance that covers the rest of their bodies. Bats have wings that are made of skin, while birds have wings made of feathers.

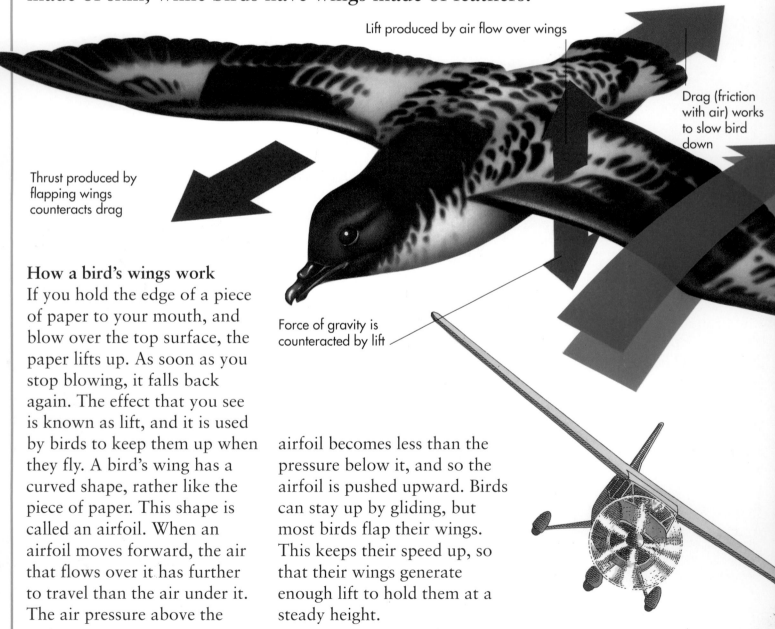

Lift produced by air flow over wings

Drag (friction with air) works to slow bird down

Thrust produced by flapping wings counteracts drag

Force of gravity is counteracted by lift

How a bird's wings work
If you hold the edge of a piece of paper to your mouth, and blow over the top surface, the paper lifts up. As soon as you stop blowing, it falls back again. The effect that you see is known as lift, and it is used by birds to keep them up when they fly. A bird's wing has a curved shape, rather like the piece of paper. This shape is called an airfoil. When an airfoil moves forward, the air that flows over it has further to travel than the air under it. The air pressure above the airfoil becomes less than the pressure below it, and so the airfoil is pushed upward. Birds can stay up by gliding, but most birds flap their wings. This keeps their speed up, so that their wings generate enough lift to hold them at a steady height.

Gliding through the forest

A flying squirrel is like a living hang glider. It has a flap of loose skin along each side of its body, and it can stretch out the flaps so that they make a big, flat surface. The squirrel can glide for about 80 yards (75m) if it launches itself from a high tree. Flying squirrels live in the forests of Central Africa.

Bats

Bats are the only mammals that can fly using muscle power. A bat's wing opens like an umbrella, and it has a sheet of skin that is stretched out between incredibly long and thin finger bones. When the bat lands, it either folds its wings, or wraps them around its body. Most bats feed on insects, and some catch their food by knocking it into the flap of skin between their back legs and tail.

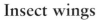

Insect wings

Butterflies have 2 pairs of flat, stiff wings. The 2 wings on each side hook together. Each wing is covered in tiny overlapping scales. A butterfly beats it wings about 5 times a second.

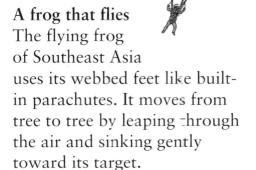

A frog that flies

The flying frog of Southeast Asia uses its webbed feet like built-in parachutes. It moves from tree to tree by leaping through the air and sinking gently toward its target.

Escape into the air

If a flying fish is being chased, it uses surprise tactics and bursts up through the water's surface. The fish glides by spreading out its very long pectoral fins. It sometimes gathers speed by trailing part of its tail in the water and flapping it from side to side. A flying fish can only stay airborne for a few seconds, but this may be long enough.

Flying on silk

A newly hatched spider has a special way of moving from one place to another. It climbs to the top of a plant stem, and then makes a thread of silk which is so fine that it snakes away in the breeze. As the thread gets longer, it begins to tug at the spider. Eventually the spider is carried high into the sky.

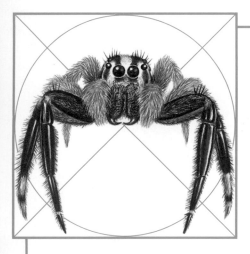

EYES AND EARS

All animals use their senses to stay up-to-date with the world around them. The senses of touch and taste tell them about things that are nearby. Three other senses—smell, hearing and vision—tell them about things that are further away. For hunters, these 3 senses are very important. The jumping spider will turn toward your finger if you move it near him, looking to see if it is good to eat.

An owl's forward-pointing eyes give it "binocular vision," so that it can judge distances

Gathering light

An eye is a sense organ that detects light. The simplest eyes can only sense the difference between light and dark, but complicated eyes (like ours) form a detailed picture. They do this like a camera, by using a lens to focus light onto a special screen, called a retina. The retina is packed with nerve cells that sense the light and produce an image. Our eyes have many nerve cells that make a color image in bright light. An owl's cells work better in dim light.

Upside-down image

Iris changes shape to adjust amount of light entering eye

Lens

Human eye

Retina

Camera

Lens

Diaphragm

Upside-down image

Film

Hunting by sound

Bats hunt by making pulses of very high-pitched sounds. A bat follows the echoes from flying insects to trap them. This system is called echolocation. Ships use a similar system, called sonar, to track submarines or chart the ocean floor.

Sound bounces back from flying insect

Bat sends out pulses of high-pitched sound

Echo from submarine or ocean floor

Pulses of sound from ship

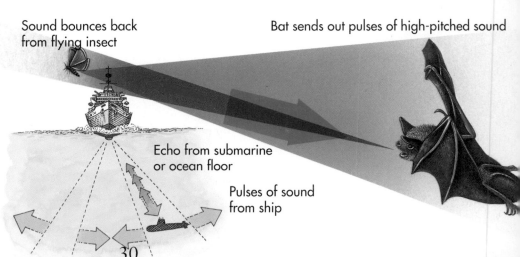

30

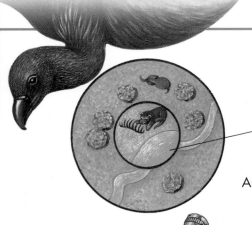

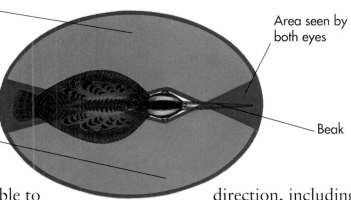

Area seen by left eye

Highly detailed image

Area seen by right eye

Area seen by both eyes

Beak

Eyes in the sky

Vultures can see food from high up in the air. Their eyes are packed with nerve cells, so they see detail greater than a human could. Vultures also keep an eye on each other. If one flies down to feed, others follow from far off.

All-round view

Imagine being able to see all around yourself without moving your head. The snipe is a small bird that does this all the time. It eyes face in exactly opposite directions, so that it can see danger from any direction, including above. The view from its 2 eyes slightly overlaps in front, behind and overhead, making it a very difficult bird to catch!

Compound image from left eye

Compound image from right eye

Dots add together to form a picture

Eyes along edge of shell

On the lookout

A scallop has many small eyes around the edge of its shell, warning it if another animal comes close. It then shuts its shell.

Compound eyes

Dragonflies catch other insects in mid-air. They hunt by sight, using large "compound" eyes made of hundreds of separate units. Each unit has a lens, and it produces a tiny image. The dragonfly's brain puts the images

together like dots on a television screen to make an overall picture.

Shaken by sound

Sound is made up of waves of pressure that travel through air. When they hit an eardrum, it vibrates. Nerve cells in the ear detect the vibrations, and a sound is heard. Our eardrums are inside our skulls. A frog's are outside.

Ears everywhere

Grasshoppers and crickets have eardrums on the sides of their bodies or on their legs.

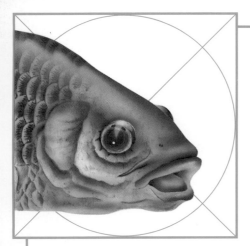

LUNGS AND GILLS

Animals need oxygen in order to survive. Without it, their cells cannot work. For a very small animal, getting oxygen is quite easy. The oxygen simply spreads into its body from outside, while a waste gas called carbon dioxide spreads in the other direction. Larger animals use gills, lungs or special tubes to gather oxygen from outside. Their blood system carries it around their bodies and collects waste carbon dioxide to expel.

Getting enough oxygen
Although we cannot see it, oxygen is all around us. It makes up part of the atmosphere, and it also dissolves in water. Oxygen gets into animals by spreading or "diffusing" through a surface. As you can see below, small objects have a relatively large surface compared to their volume. But large objects have a relatively small surface and need lungs or gills to let enough oxygen in.

Flatworm

Oxygen diffuses in to reach all the parts of the body

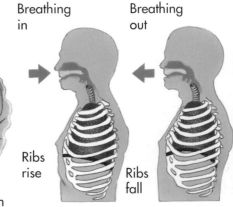

Breathing in   Breathing out

Ribs rise   Ribs fall

Human lungs
Your lungs are rather like sponges. They have a very large surface area packed into a relatively small volume. When you breathe in, your ribs lift upwards and your diaphragm falls, making your lungs expand. This sucks air down your trachea (windpipe), filling the lungs. The air travels through a network of branching passages, until it finally reaches millions of tiny dead-end passages called alveoli. Oxygen from the air passes through the walls of the alveoli into the blood.

	Surface area	Volume	Area/volume
⬜	6	1	6
⬜	24	8	3
⬜	54	27	2

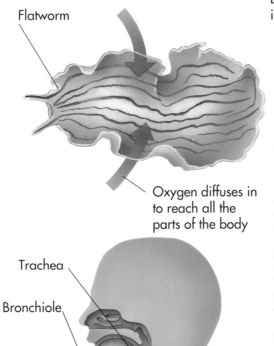

Trachea

Bronchiole

Lung

Bronchus   Diaphragm

A living snorkel

The larva (grub) of a mosquito grows up in water, but it breathes air. It does this by using a special tube that works like a snorkel. The larva floats just beneath the surface, with its tube touching the surface. The tube has a fringe of hairs which repel water, so it does not get wet inside. If danger threatens, the larva wriggles away from the surface, and the hairs close the tube's tip.

A breathing book

A spider breathes through "book lungs," which are packed into the underside of its abdomen. A book lung is made of many small body flaps, separated by narrow air spaces. Air flows into the spaces, and oxygen can diffuse through the flaps to reach the spider's blood. Some spiders also have air-tubes running through their bodies, rather like those of insects.

Oxygen spread to rest of body

Air space with support pillars

Air flows in

Book lung

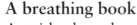

Oxygen for flight

Birds are very active animals, and they use up oxygen quickly. Their lungs are very good at gathering oxygen, because air flows through them in one direction. When a bird takes a breath, the air travels into special cavities, called air sacs. It then flows through the lungs and into another set of sacs before being breathed out.

Water flow

Vein

Artery

Gill arch

Gill flap

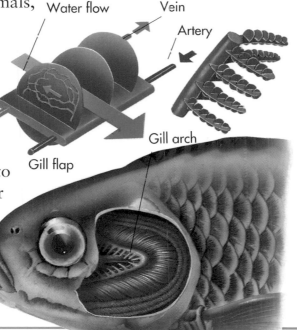

Air-filled insects

Insects do not use blood to carry oxygen. Instead, their bodies are filled with air-filled tubes. Each tube, or "trachea," starts at a special porthole, called a spiracle. This can be opened or closed. It branches out to reach individual cells.

Trachea

Air sacs

Lungs

Breathing in water

Fish cannot breathe air, but they need oxygen just as much as we do. They get their oxygen from water, by using gills. As water moves through a fish's gills, it flows past rows of tiny flaps containing blood vessels. The blood takes up the water's oxygen, and carries it around the body.

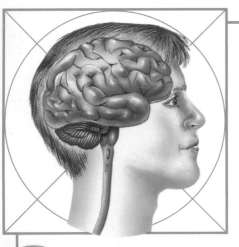

NERVES AND BRAIN

If you touch an earthworm on its tail, it will quickly pull it in and crawl away. Like those of all animals, its rapid reactions are controlled by nerves. Nerves are bundles of neurons—long, thin cells that carry electrical signals. There are 3 main kinds of neuron: sensory neurons, motor neurons and association neurons.

Brain

Spinal cord

Cell body

Impulse passes down axon

Direction of impulse

Insulating cells

Motor

Wire

Nerve signal (impulse) received from neighboring nerve by dendrite

On/off switch

Battery

Electrical circuit

Nerves carrying signals to and from leg

The human nervous system

Your nervous system is one of the most important control systems in your body. It is made of 2 parts. The peripheral nervous system carries nerve signals to and from all parts of your body. Your central nervous system (CNS), which includes your brain and spinal cord, monitors these signals and issues signals itself. The signals or "impulses" travel along neurons rather like an electrical current flowing along a wire.

Reflexes

When an animal steps on something sharp, its nervous system automatically makes it pull away. This is a reflex reaction. Reflexes work very quickly, because they involve very few neurons. A sensory neuron detects pain, and sends a signal to the spinal cord. Here, an association neuron triggers a motor neuron, which makes a muscle contract.

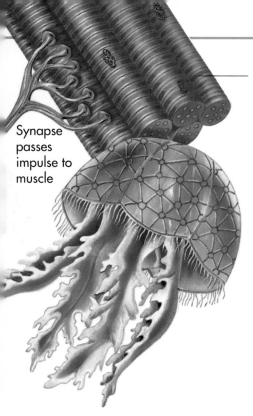

Synapse passes impulse to muscle

Muscle contracts

Amphibian

Reptile

Bird

Mammal

Human

Cerebellum

Cerebrum

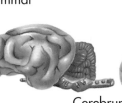

Net of nerves

A jellyfish has a simple nervous system, like most invertebrates. Most of its neurons are spread out in a net, but some ring its bell-shaped body. These neurons produce impulses at set intervals, contracting muscles to make the jellyfish swim.

Association neuron passes signal to motor neuron

Motor neuron makes leg move

Pain produces signal in sensory neuron

Brains

A brain is an animal's control center. It is made of millions of neurons, packed tightly together. When the brain works, countless signals flash through this network of cells, following any one of billions of possible pathways. Different parts of the brain specialize in different tasks, and the shape of an animal's brain mirrors the way that it lives. The *medulla* controls some reflexes and links the brain with the spinal cord. The *cerebellum* coordinates balance and movement, while the *cerebrum* processes information. In

Chemical messengers

Nerves are not the only way that your body gets messages from one place to another. If you get a fright, cells above your kidneys release a chemical messenger or "hormone" called adrenaline. This quickly flows around your bloodstream and makes you ready to react to danger.

humans, the cerebrum is unusually well developed, so that it covers most of the other parts of the brain. Despite its size, the human brain is not the largest in the animal world. That record goes to the sperm whale, whose brain can weigh seven times that of an adult man.

Rapid reaction

An earthworm's nervous system is "wired up" to respond quickly if its tail is touched. It has giant nerve fibers that run along its body. These fibers carry nervous impulses very quickly, so the worm can pull its tail away if danger threatens.

Rings of nerve cells around body cavity

Nerve cord running along underside

MUSCLES

A car engine works by pushing. The pistons push outward through the cylinders, and this turns a camshaft which powers the wheels. Muscles work the other way around. When a muscle receives signals from a nerve, it shortens. This makes it pull or squeeze part of the body so that it moves. Muscles make up an important part of most animals. Half the weight of your body is muscle.

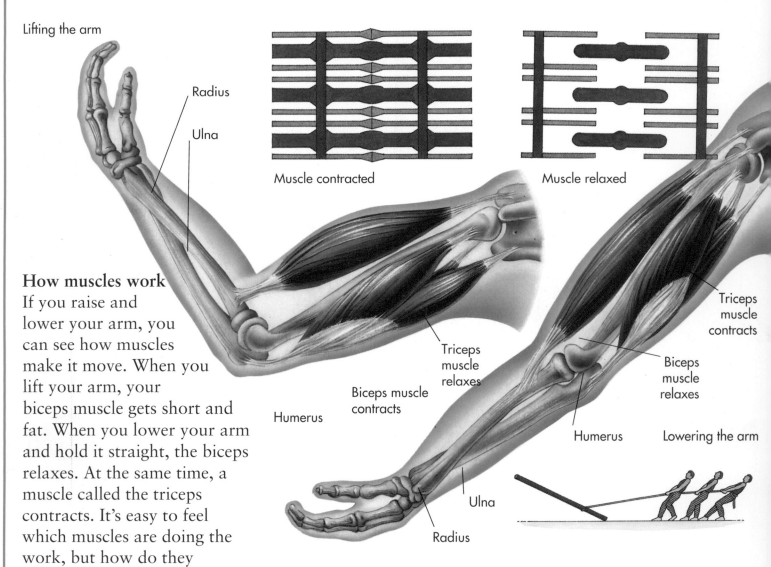

Lifting the arm

Radius

Ulna

Muscle contracted

Muscle relaxed

Triceps muscle relaxes

Biceps muscle contracts

Humerus

Triceps muscle contracts

Biceps muscle relaxes

Humerus

Lowering the arm

Ulna

Radius

How muscles work
If you raise and lower your arm, you can see how muscles make it move. When you lift your arm, your biceps muscle gets short and fat. When you lower your arm and hold it straight, the biceps relaxes. At the same time, a muscle called the triceps contracts. It's easy to feel which muscles are doing the work, but how do they contract? If a muscle cell is magnified many times, it usually shows a pattern of stripes. These stripes are formed by 2 sets of chemicals,

arranged like layers in a sandwich. When nerves tell the muscle to contract, the chemicals attract each other, and the muscle shortens. Not

all muscles are exactly like this. "Involuntary" muscles, like those in your heart and intestines, work without your telling them to.

36

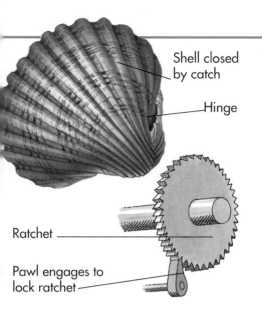

Shell closed by catch

Hinge

Ratchet

Pawl engages to lock ratchet

The spring-loaded flea

Muscles contract too slowly to power the flea's amazing jump. Instead, the flea uses its muscles indirectly. The muscles gradually squash a special pad behind each leg, and when the flea jumps, it releases the energy stored in the pads. Its legs suddenly flick backward, and the flea hurtles into the air.

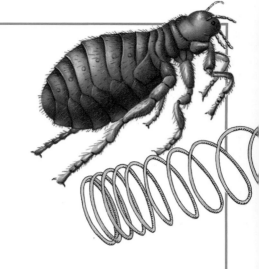

A muscle that locks

Bivalve mollusks, like the cockle, protect themselves by shutting their shells. Their shells are made of 2 parts joined by a hinge. A powerful muscle is attached to each part of the shell, and when this contracts, the shell shuts. Bivalve mollusks can keep their shells shut for hours without tiring because the shell muscle can "lock" shut.

Non-stop pump

Your heart is made of a special kind of muscle, and it beats about 100,000 times a day. It consists of 2 pumps. One side pumps blood to the lungs. The blood then returns to the other side of the heart to be pumped around the body. The heart has valves, to keep blood from flowing the wrong way.

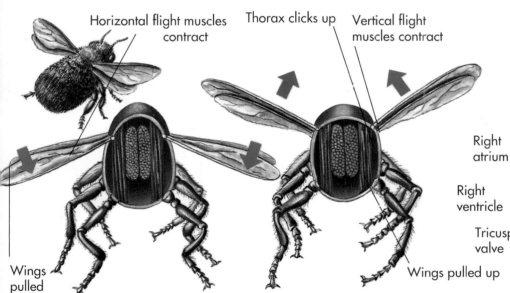

Horizontal flight muscles contract

Thorax clicks up

Vertical flight muscles contract

Wings pulled down

Wings pulled up

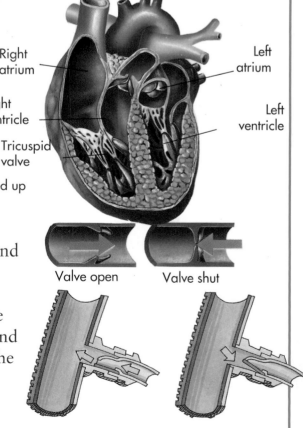

Right atrium

Right ventricle

Tricuspid valve

Left atrium

Left ventricle

Valve open

Valve shut

How bees fly

A bumblebee uses 2 sets of muscles to fly. But strange though it sounds, none of these muscles are attached directly to its wings. Instead, the muscles pull against the bee's thorax (the middle part of its body). One set pulls the thorax from front to back, and one set pulls it from top to bottom. These muscles take turns contracting, so that the top of the thorax clicks up and down like the lid on a tin. The wings are attached to the thorax and beat when the thorax changes shape.

NESTS

A nest is a special shelter that parent animals build to protect their young. Most people know that birds make nests, but so do many other kinds of animals. They include bees and wasps, and also spiders, reptiles and mammals. Some fish even make nests underwater. The simplest nests are built in just a few minutes, but more complicated ones can take days or weeks. Even when a nest is finished, the work may not be over. If a male weaverbird cannot attract a mate to the nest he has built, he gives it up and starts all over again.

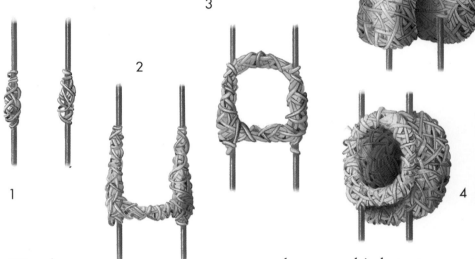

1 2 3 4 5

Nest materials
Birds use many different materials to make their nests, including sticks, moss, feathers, and even pieces of paper or string. Each kind of bird uses its materials in a particular way. Most finches build a cup-shaped nest.

Weaving a nest
Weaving is a way of making something strong out of something flexible. We use weaving to make baskets and fabrics, and in nature some animals use it to make nests. A male weaverbird starts a nest by tying grass to 2 nearby branches (1). It then weaves a bridge between them (2), and makes a loop (3). It can now weave the egg chamber (4), and finally the entrance (5).

Grass

Lichen

Leaves

Hair or wool

Moss

Wasp nests

A wasp nest is like a miniature high-rise building made of paper. It has lots of floors, separated by spaces, and it is enclosed by a protective shell. The whole nest hangs from a branch or roof-beam.

Inside the nest

Each floor of a wasp nest is made of many 6-sided cells packed together to form a "comb." The cells are where the young wasps grow up. The queen wasp lays an egg in each cell, and worker wasps feed the growing grubs.

Making paper

Humans did not really "invent" paper, because wasps have been using it for far longer than we have. Paper is made from tiny fibers of dead wood, mixed into a wet pulp and then spread out to dry. We make paper using heavy machinery, but a wasp can do the same thing using its jaws

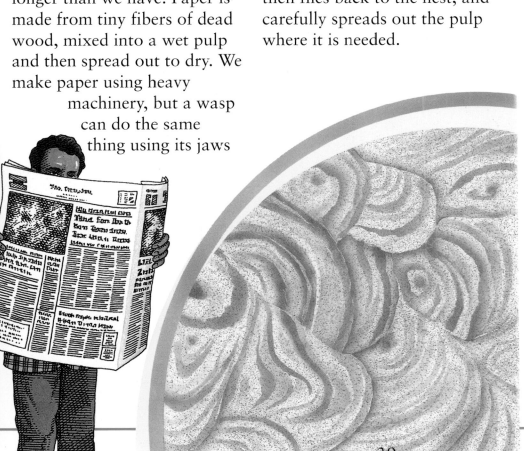

and its saliva. It scrapes wood fibers from bark or fence-posts, and chews them up. It then flies back to the nest, and carefully spreads out the pulp where it is needed.

Stick-on nest

The cave swiftlet makes its nest from sticky saliva. It begins by glueing a blob of saliva to a cave wall. It then works outward to form a small cup. As the saliva dries, it hardens.

Buried in the sand

Turtles lay their eggs on sandy beaches. The turtle digs a hole with her flippers. After laying, she carefully covers the nest with sand.

Nests on stilts

The female field mouse makes her ball-shaped nest by weaving blades of grass around sturdy grass stems. The nest does not have an entrance —the mouse simply pushes her way in.

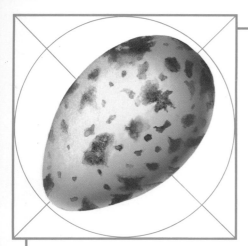

EGGS

An egg is a special cell that develops to form a young animal. The original cell that makes up the egg soon begins to divide. It does this many times, until there are millions or even billions of new cells. The new cells make different layers, and these fold up and change shape. After days or weeks, a new animal body begins to form. All animals that reproduce by mating have eggs.

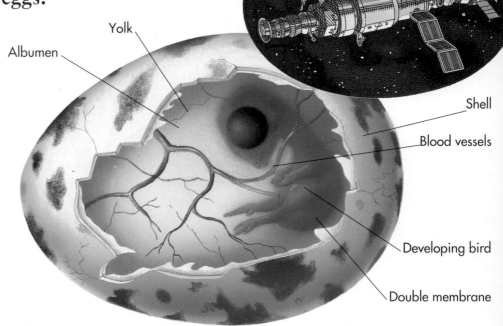

Yolk
Albumen
Shell
Blood vessels
Developing bird
Double membrane

A protecting shell

Like a space-station orbiting the Earth, a bird's egg contains everything that its passenger needs to survive. The egg contains lots of yolk, which is a private food supply for the developing bird. The egg white, or albumen, holds a store of water. The shell around the egg keeps it from losing too much water, but lets in oxygen.

Human development

A human being starts life when a male cell fertilizes an egg cell inside the mother's body. The egg cell begins to divide, and it forms a hollow ball called a blastocyst. The blastocyst settles on the lining of the mother's uterus, or womb, and it burrows into it. Once it has become "implanted," it is nourished by food substances from the mother's blood. These move into its blood through an organ called the placenta. The blood reaches the embryo through the umbilical cord. As the embryo develops, it is surrounded by fluid held inside a membrane. The fluid works like a shock absorber. Eighteen weeks after the egg cell first divided, a baby is taking shape.

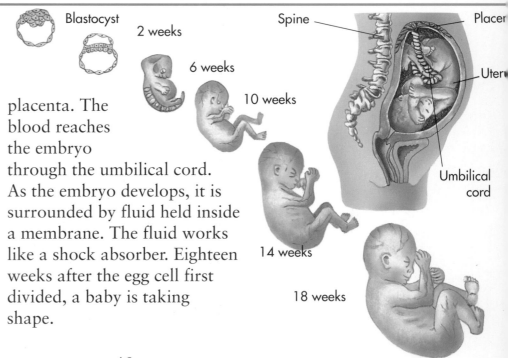

Blastocyst
2 weeks
6 weeks
10 weeks
Spine
Placen
Uter
14 weeks
Umbilical cord
18 weeks

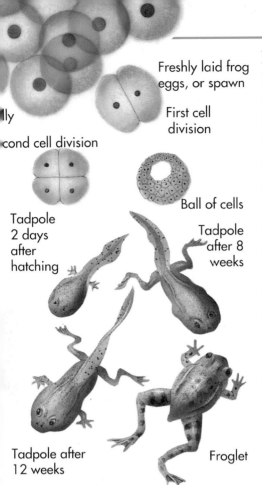

Freshly laid frog eggs, or spawn

First cell division

...ly

...cond cell division

Ball of cells

Tadpole 2 days after hatching

Tadpole after 8 weeks

Tadpole after 12 weeks

Froglet

Frogspawn

Frogs and toads spend much of their lives on land, but they have to return to water to lay their eggs. The eggs are quite small when they are laid, but they quickly absorb water and this gives them a thick coating of jelly. The single cell divides many times to form a ball of cells, and from this a tadpole slowly takes shape. The tadpole eventually swims free from the jelly, and starts to feed on tiny plants. As it gets older, it becomes a meat-eater and develops legs. Once the tadpole has absorbed its tail, it is ready for life on land.

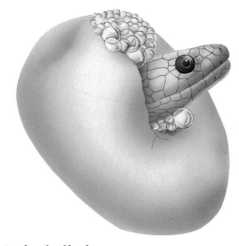

Soft-shelled eggs

A snake's egg has a soft, leathery, waterproof shell. Some snakes develop and hatch inside their mother's body.

Butterfly eggs

If you look closely at leaves during the spring and summer, you may see little clusters of eggs laid by butterflies. When a caterpillar hatches from its egg, it often eats the shell.

Mermaid's purse

This strangely shaped object is a "mermaid's purse," or the egg of a dogfish. Its long tendrils wrap around seaweed. The whale shark, a distant relative lays a purse 1 foot (30cm) long.

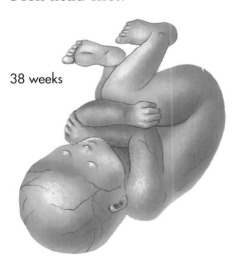

Preparing for birth

By the end of the 22nd week, the baby's skeleton has formed, and its joints are developing. By the time the baby is ready to be born, after about 38 weeks, it fills its

mother's uterus, and is curled up tightly. Most babies are born head-first.

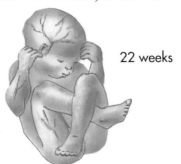

22 weeks

38 weeks

Egg-laying mammals

The duck-billed platypus is a mammal that lays eggs. Platypuses live in Australia, and use their bills to collect food from river beds.

41

BURROWS AND SHELTERS

The ground beneath our feet is a hidden world that we know little about. But for many animals, it is a place of safety and even a source of food. Life underground has its advantages. It is harder for predators to launch a surprise attack below ground, and the underground "climate" stays much the same, whatever the weather above. Most animals that live underground dig their way through the soil, but the earthworm eats its way along.

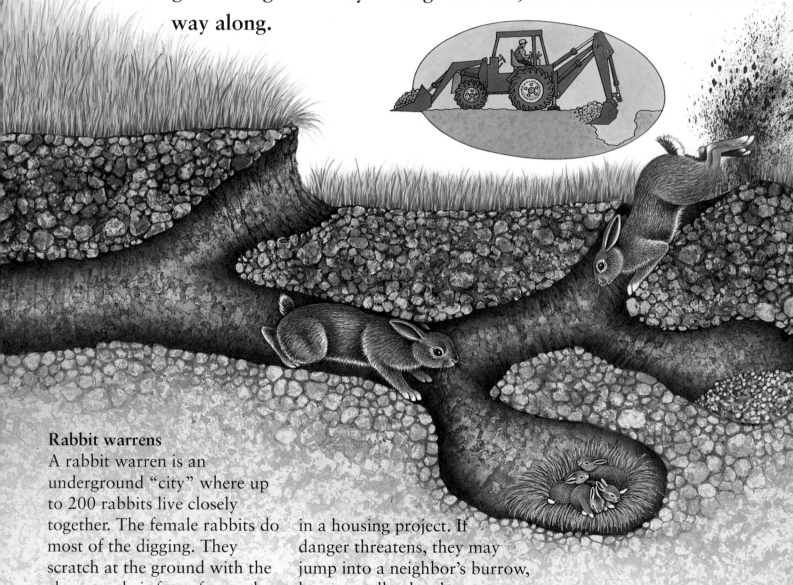

Rabbit warrens
A rabbit warren is an underground "city" where up to 200 rabbits live closely together. The female rabbits do most of the digging. They scratch at the ground with the claws on their front feet and then shovel the loose earth backward. In most warrens, the rabbits live in their own tunnels, rather like neighbors in a housing project. If danger threatens, they may jump into a neighbor's burrow, but generally, they keep to their own. Each female gives birth to up to 9 young in a special nest chamber that she lines with grass and fur.

Rabbits are blind and hairless at birth. A mother may have 2 or 3 families a year, but many young are killed by predators.

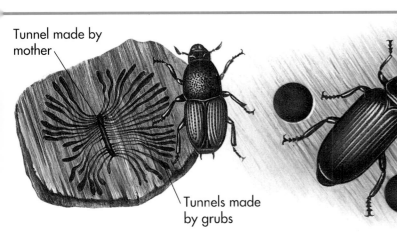

Tunnel made by mother

Tunnels made by grubs

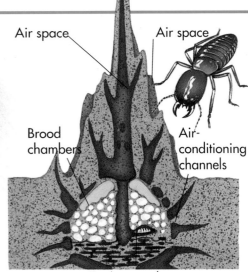

Air space

Air space

Brood chambers

Air-conditioning channels

Fungus garden

Burrowing through bark

If you pull a piece of bark from a dead tree, you may see patterns on the underside. These are "galleries" made by bark beetles. The female lays eggs along one tunnel and the grubs burrow their own.

Woodworm

A woodworm is the grub of a small beetle. It chews its way through wood, and digests the food that it contains. After many months, the grub turns into an adult beetle. It chews a hole through the wood and crawls out to seek a mate.

Gardens below ground

Termites are small insects that live together in enormous family groups. Some build huge nests, where they grow a kind of fungus in special underground gardens. They eat parts of it as it grows.

Mole patrol

A mole spends nearly all its life underground. It digs long tunnels with its spade-like front feet. It presses some of the soil against the sides of the tunnels, and piles up the rest above ground in "molehills." The mole patrols up and down, feeling and smelling for worms and insects that have dropped into its tunnels.

Tunneling through food

An earthworm eats its way through the soil like a tunneling machine. When it swallows, the soil passes through into a body chamber, called a gizzard, where it is ground up. The worm extracts any food from the soil, and the rest passes out in the form of "worm casts" on the surface of the ground.

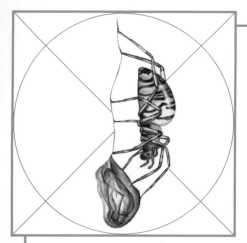

WEBS AND OTHER TRAPS

For small animals, the world is full of unpleasant surprises. Camouflaged hunters are always ready to ambush the unwary, and nature's trap-makers wait patiently for their prey. The trappers include many different kinds of animal, but one group—the spiders—stands out above all others. Spiders make their webs and traps using silk. They make and store the silk in liquid form, but when they squeeze the liquid out of their bodies, it becomes solid. A silk strand is stretchy and almost completely transparent. It is also very strong.

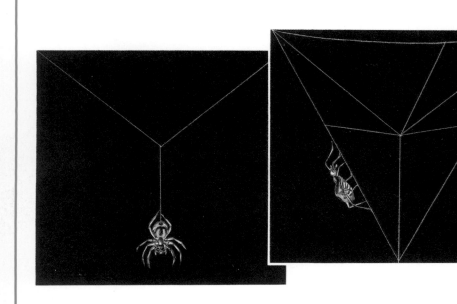

Spinning a web
An orb-web spider makes its nest by stretching strong threads of dry silk between solid supports, like branches or the corner of a window frame. It then adds a spiral of silk that contains thousands of tiny droplets of glue. When an insect flies into the web, the spider detects the vibrations that it produces. It runs over the web, and gives its victim a deadly bite.

A spider has curved claws which hook over the silk threads of its web

Sticky snare
The bolas spider does not spin a web. Instead, it makes a thread of silk that is tipped with a blob of glue. The thread works just like a fly-paper. The spider whirls it in a circle, so that it catches flying insects.

Hunters in flowers

Every day, millions of insects visit flowers to find food. This makes flowers a perfect place to launch a deadly ambush. Two kinds of animals specialize in this kind of hunting, and both are brightly colored so that they blend in with their background. Crab spiders sit on or underneath flowers. If an insect comes within range, a crab spider lunges forward and catches it. Flower mantises wait on top of the flower with their stabbing front legs at the ready.

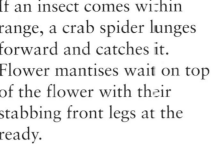

A hidden trapdoor

A trapdoor spider digs a vertical tunnel in the ground and lines it with silk. It also uses silk to make a watertight trapdoor, which fits neatly over the tunnel's entrance. The spider then lies in wait, with the door slightly open, and 2 of its legs sticking out. If an insect walks past and touches the door, the spider pulls it into the tunnel and shuts the door tightly.

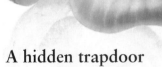
Silk lining   Silk trapdoor

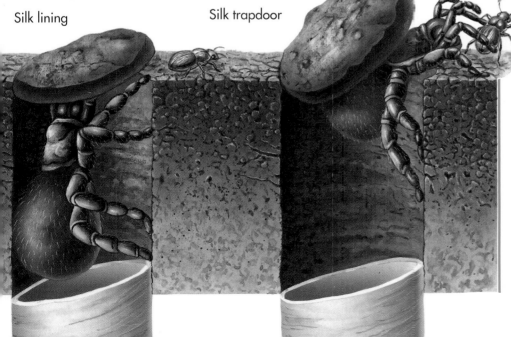

Fishing in the dark

Angler fish live in deep water, far beyond the reach of sunlight. They have a built-in lure which glows in the dark. If a fish comes too close to the lure, the angler snaps it up.

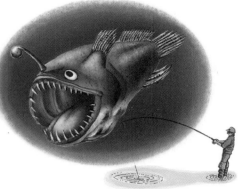

One false step

An ant-lion grub digs a steep-sided pit, and buries itself at the bottom, with only its jaws showing. If an ant walks past, the ant-lion flicks earth at it till it falls in.

Fishing nets

The grubs of caddisflies live in water. One kind weaves itself a silk web, and lies in wait in the web's narrow neck.

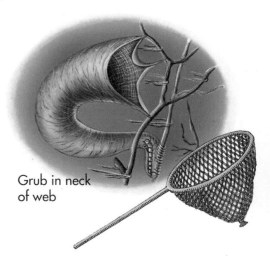
Grub in neck of web

INDEX